Making a Splash!

Baptist Union
of Great Britain

www.baptist.org.uk

Published on behalf of The Baptist Union of Great Britain
by Nigel Lynn Publishing & Marketing Ltd
106 High Street, Milton under Wychwood, Chipping Norton
Oxfordshire OX7 6ET, United Kingdom
enquiries@nigellynnpublishing.com

The Baptist Union of Great Britain
Baptist House, 129 Broadway, Didcot
Oxfordshire OX11 8RT, United Kingdom

First published 2007

British Library Cataloguing in Publication Data
Data available

ISBN   978 0 901472 49 6

3 5 7 9 10 8 6 4 2

Printed in the United Kingdom by
Goodman Baylis Ltd, Worcester

Contents

Acknowledgements

This book has been produced by BUGB's Mission Department, with grateful thanks to:

- Helen Bellamy, Claire Earl, Gary Bott and Andy Levett for their hard work and inspiration in writing the sections.
- All those who have willingly allowed us to use photographs of their baptisms.
- Dave Walker for the inspiration behind his cartoons.
- Paul Brown Imaging for the cover photograph.

Scripture taken from *The Message*. Copyright © 1993, 1994, 1995, 1996, 2000, 2001, 2002. Used by permission of NavPress Publishing Group.

Exploring your faith

When you are baptised you will probably be asked several questions about what you believe. They may not be exactly the same as the questions below, but will probably be something like:

> 'Do you believe in one God, Father, Son and Holy Spirit?'
> (You answer) *'I do'*
> 'Do you confess Jesus Christ as your Lord and Saviour?'
> *'I do.'*
> 'Do you turn from sin, renounce evil and intend to follow Christ?'
> *'I do.'*
> 'Will you live within the fellowship of the church and will you serve Jesus Christ in the world?'
> *'I will'*

These questions and answers come from the Baptist Union of Great Britain's book *Gathering for Worship*. We're going to explore these questions so that you understand more about what being a Christian is all about.

'Do you believe in one God, Father, Son and Holy Spirit?'

Believe

If you have to cross a river and there's a bridge nearby no amount of engineering knowledge and bridge-building expertise will get you across. You have to use the bridge and walk across.

Being a Christian is not about what you

know, but who you know. Knowing about Jesus is different from putting your faith in him. Some people can remember a moment in their life when they prayed a prayer and put their faith in Jesus. Others can't remember a special moment, but they do know that they are a believer. Both are ways of becoming a Christian, and neither is better than the other.

It's a bit like going from England to Scotland. If you go on the motorway you will go past a sign on the border that says 'Welcome to Scotland'. As you go past the sign you know you have entered a new country. However, if you are walking in the border hills and cross into Scotland it may take you some time before you realise that you have left England and are now in Scotland. You can't say exactly when you crossed into Scotland but you know that you are there now. Both are equally successful ways of getting into Scotland!

One God, Father, Son and Holy Spirit

Most people believe in a god of some description. Christians believe in God who wants to get to know us and wants us to get to know him.

Who do you get on well with? Why is this relationship special or important to you?

God wants to be the most special and important person in your life. While there are parallels between human relationships and our relationship with Jesus, there are also significant differences including the nature of Jesus' love for us (spiritual and based on unconditional selfless love, not hormonal and based on physical and emotional attraction); he is not physically with us in the same way as people around us; he doesn't let us down, unlike friends and family... The key point here is that God wants to be special and important in our lives.

Words like creator, father or powerful might come to mind. He made human beings, perfect and good. Maybe you have an image of an old man with a white beard (no, not Santa!). God is the supreme being in the universe. He made everything and is the source of life. He gave us the gift of free will to choose between

PLEASE TAKE A QUESTIONNAIRE AND FILL IT IN WHILE YOU WAIT

MARY WAS NOT EXPECTING A WRITTEN TEST AT HER BAPTIS

right and wrong. Why do we need God? People search for him because he satisfies our hunger for meaning and purpose in life, for life beyond death. More than that, we make wrong choices with the free will we've been given and need his help to sort out the mess we find ourselves in.

Who is God to you; how do you see him?

Often when we talk of God we use the pronoun 'he', but God is beyond gender. The words we use to describe God will never be good enough to give a full and complete description – he is so much more than we can ever imagine. However, he has made himself known to humans in ways that we describe as Father, Son and Spirit.

Father

No human Dad can ever live up to the ideals we set for them – we know that they let us down. At the same time, God is far more than a father – did you know that the Bible also describes God as a mother? God is our heavenly parent.

What would an ideal father be like?

However, the Bible does talk a lot about God as our heavenly father. That's how the prayer we call the 'Lord's Prayer' starts: 'Our Father in heaven...' Father God is much more than a nice dad on a cloud. Father God loves every single person completely. To describe God as 'Father' means we can be God's children. Father God is the one who imagined everything into existence – including us.

Son

Jesus is the central figure in the Christian faith, and we are named after him: 'Christ – ians'.

You may think of words like God's Son, saviour, healer or special friend. Jesus is the best way we can see what God is like – he has the family likeness! Father God sent him into the world so that people could know what he is like, so he could show people the way he wants us to live our lives, and so that he could sort out the mess caused by us failing to live that way.

The fish symbol is an early secret code that Christians used to identify one another and remind themselves of who Jesus was. They spoke ancient Greek,

What Christian symbols do you know?

and the word for fish is 'Ichthus'. When you take the letters of this word in Greek they are the first letters in the words:

I = Jesus
Ch = Christ
Th = God's
U = Son
S = Saviour

Jesus lived such an incredible life: performing such miracles and saying such amazing things that people were convinced that he was someone special. Those closest to him could tell that he was more than just a great man, he was God here on earth with us – the best way to describe him was as God's son! (Have a look at Matthew 16:13–17). We'll come back to the last word a bit later.

Holy Spirit

What do you think of when you hear the words 'Holy Spirit'?

Perhaps you think of words like counsellor, healer or guide. Maybe you don't know what to think!

When he went back to heaven Jesus did not leave us alone, he left the Holy Spirit to guide us and to give us peace. This does not mean that we no longer have a relationship with Jesus. Jesus did not only die but was raised from the dead by the Father, he is alive and lives on in the believer, (look at John 14:16–21). The Holy Spirit helps us to know what God wants us to do, he helps us to pray, he encourages us in our faith and he gives us spiritual strength. He is at work in us helping us to become more like the people God created us to be, and gives us spiritual gifts to help us be more effective in our lives.

Ok, so how can these three be one God?

There is no easy answer to this question, except to say that it's how we experience God. However, let's explore the concept a bit to make you more comfortable.

God is a relationship – Father, Son and Spirit. The Bible talks a lot about God's love. Love only exists if there is someone to love. Because God is a relationship then love is at the heart of who God is – Father, Son and Spirit love each other.

All of them share the same 'Godness', but they are distinct 'people' at the same time. If you are still confused, it may help to think in terms of 'who' and 'what'. Father, Son and Spirit are who God is; God is what they are. There is one God (that's what they are) but three 'persons' (that's who they are). It's a bit like members of the same family. However, that's a bit inadequate to describe the Trinity (the word we use to describe God being three-in-one).

Are there any things that you can think of that have three distinct parts, but are also one?

Another image that's sometimes used is that of water (appropriate in the context of baptism!). Water can be a solid (ice), liquid, or vapour (steam), but it is still all water – three in one! A tree has roots, a trunk and branches. If you are into maths, try this: $1 \times 1 \times 1 = 1$.

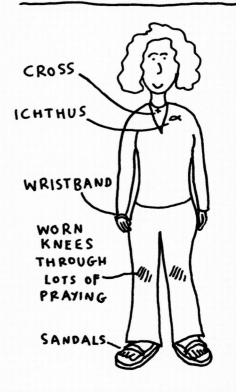

CHRISTIAN SYMBOLS

CROSS
ICHTHUS
WRISTBAND
WORN KNEES THROUGH LOTS OF PRAYING
SANDALS

'Do you confess Jesus Christ as your Lord and Saviour?'

Jesus as Lord

When you are on a bus, train or aeroplane it is encouraging to know that there is someone up front who knows what they are doing and who is in control. We are usually very happy to let them take us where we want to go.

How about your life? Saying that 'Jesus is Lord' is saying that you have decided to allow Jesus to be in charge of your life. You want to follow his teaching and live in a way that respects him. You don't want to do or say things that would upset him.

Jesus as Saviour

Remember the fish symbol and the last word represented in the Greek word 'Ichthus'? Jesus is described as 'Saviour'. That assumes that there is something we need to be saved from. Another

What means of execution can you think of?

significant Christian symbol is a cross. It may seem bizarre that we would use a method of cruel execution like that – it's a bit like using an electric chair or firing squad. If you read Matthew 16:21 you can see that Jesus was saying that his death was going to be significant. In fact it is the most significant event in human history – it's how he saved us.

Remember the way in which God made us – with a free will to decide what to do. Because we don't always make the right choice we fall short of God's standard of perfection. God, who is perfect, can't have anything to do with imperfection so our messing things up separates us from God.

There is no historical doubt that Jesus was crucified by Romans at the request of the religious leaders of his day. There's plenty of historical evidence (not just the Bible) that within three days he had been raised back to life! This is the most significant event in human history because it resolves the problems caused by our failing to live up to God's standards. Let's look at some images that describe the problem:

1. *It is like we are a criminal who has rightly been convicted of a crime and condemned to death.* God's justice means someone has to pay for the crime. Jesus died in our place, even though we deserved to die. Because our sentence has been carried out there is no longer anything to separate us from God.

2. *It is as if we owe God a huge debt and could never pay it ourselves.* The debt that was owed has been paid by Jesus when he died. We no longer owe God anything.

3. *Our failure is like a dirty stain we can never clean off.* Jesus' death is like the most powerful soap ever that washes us completely clean.

4. *Letting God down is like we have let down a really close friend and wrecked our relationship.* Jesus' death shows us how much God loves us. Even though he is the injured party he offers to forgive us completely and restore the broken relationship. That forgiveness can set us free from guilt about our past.

5. *Evil in the world needs to be defeated.* The most visible sign of evil is death. When Jesus died it was as if evil had won, but his resurrection shows that God is in charge and he has defeated the forces of evil.

6. *Without God we are hopelessly lost and can't find him.* God has come to the world to find us. Jesus' death is like a beacon in the darkness that shows us where God is.

7. *The things we do that disappoint God are like chains that bind us and restrict us from reaching out to God.* Jesus' death was such a powerful event that it broke the chains and set us free to be with God

At the heart of all these images is that God loves us so much that he sent Jesus into the world to sort out the problems we have caused which separate us from him. He offers forgiveness and to make things right between us and God.

'Do you turn from sin, renounce evil and intend to follow Christ?'

Sin?

Imagine an archery target in which you are required to hit the bull's-eye. That is the standard of perfection that God wants in our lives. In medieval

times an arrow that didn't reach the target was called a 'sin arrow'. Our problem is that the way we live often doesn't even come close to hitting the target, never mind the bull's-eye! That's sin. The things we say, think and do that upset God have their root in a wrong attitude within us – 'sin'. 'Sin' is the old-fashioned word that is used to describe the many ways in which people fall short of God's standards. Sin hurts people, including God and us, as it breaks down relationships. Sin cuts you off from God in this life and the one to come.

What happens when you put two north poles of magnets together?

Like poles of a magnet repel each other – they can't exist together. That's what our sin does to God. Because he is so perfect he can't have anything sinful in his presence, so we are repelled. All sins are equally disgusting to God (that's the bad news) but all sins can be forgiven when we give them to Jesus to deal with (that's the good news).

In Matthew 22:37–38 we read of Jesus pointing out that the most important commandment is to love God completely. We sin when we do not do that, and when we decide to do what we want instead of putting God first.

Renouncing evil

To renounce something is to declare that you don't want anything to do with it from now on. It's a bit like giving something up as a new year's resolution (although hopefully it lasts a bit longer than most resolutions). You are saying that you are giving up the things that are spiritually unhealthy for you.

Giving up evil is difficult if you don't replace it with something. Following Jesus is what Christians try to do. We try to do what he says in the Bible, we try to live in a way that shows that we respect him. You can get wrist bands that have the letters 'WWJD' on them, which means 'What Would Jesus Do?' Following Jesus means that question is important to us and we try to do what he would do.

Becoming a Christian is a change of direction. It's as if you used to face away from God (towards evil) and were going in that direction. Then, when you decided to follow Jesus (see 'renouncing evil') you turned around and are headed in God's direction. There is another old-fashioned word that is sometimes used to describe this change of direction – repentance.

> *'Will you live within the fellowship of the church and will you serve Jesus Christ in the world?'*

Live in church?

'Church' is the word used to describe a group of people following Jesus – we are a church of believers. The first part of this question is not asking you to move all your stuff down to the church building (if you have one) so you can live there. It's a reminder that it is very difficult for Christians to live as Jesus wants when we are on our own.

What words can you think of that describe a group of people or things? Examples would be a herd of cattle or a flock of seagulls.

'Church' can also be a verb (action word) because it is what happens when Christians get together to do what Jesus calls us to do.

When geese are flying together, they fly in a V shape because they can fly 70% further together than they can go on their own. When you have a barbecue (with real coals, not a gas one!) if you took a coal away from the rest it would soon go

out and go cold. It's only when they are together that the heat generated keeps them going.

In the same way, being a Christian is much easier when you are with a group of other Christians who will encourage, support and look after you. A lot of the New Testament is about how Christians should be together.

For discussion:
What do you think would be some of the important parts of church life? Do these things have to be done the way we've always done them to be valid? Are there things that happen in your church that you don't think are essential? Can you offer alternatives to your church leaders that would be more relevant to you and your friends?

Serve Jesus Christ in the world

Christians should not simply stick together and ignore everyone else. Quite the opposite in fact – we are called to tell other people about Jesus and to help them.

Loving our neighbour as ourselves includes friends, family and even those we might consider to be enemies. This does not mean we have to go out of our way to be friends with everyone, as that sometimes might put you in danger.

What does the story of the 'Good Samaritan' (Luke 10:25–37) tell you about how Jesus thinks we should relate to other people? How can you show care and respect to people?

Why get baptised?

You might be thinking: 'What's the point? I'm a good (and clean) enough Christian?' You might be saying you want to get baptised because your best friend is getting baptised. Perhaps you don't know exactly why you want to get baptised – it just feels right. In this section we're going to explore some reasons for being baptised.

Reason 1:   You're in good company

For more than 2000 years people have come to faith in Christ and have been baptised by full immersion in water or by other means, including sheets and dirt where no water is available! Billions of people have gone through an act that is really one big bath (don't worry, they don't all use the same water!), and you would be joining them.

Reason 2:   It means something

The physical act of being immersed into the water reminds us of Jesus dying and being put in the tomb. We are identifying with him: some baptismal pools look like open graves. Going under the water (even though it's a short time) also reminds us that by following Jesus we have killed off our old way of life – one where we put what we wanted before what Jesus wanted.

Coming up out of the water shows that by following Jesus we have started a new life. Just like Jesus was raised from the dead so we are raised up from under the water.

Usually you change your clothes (in private) after you have been baptised which is one of the ways the Bible describes the change that takes place when you are a Christian – taking off what was wrong and putting on what is good. (Have a look at Ephesians 4:22–24, or Colossians 3:12)

People are usually baptised in front of the rest of the church, not in private. This reminds us that because we belong to God, Christians belong to each other in the same way that family members belong to each other.

IT IS GOOD TO KNOW THAT BILLIONS OF PEOPLE HAVE GONE BEFORE YOU INTO THE WATERS OF BAPTISM

Reason 3: It does something

Something happens when you are baptised – more than getting very wet! Being baptised is part of being a Christian. There is more happening than a symbolic act. If you remember from section 1, Christians are people who have made a significant change in their life – turning from putting themselves or other things first in their life towards putting God first. Have another look at that section if you are not sure about that.

You could say that there is a process of becoming a Christian (whether or not

you were aware of it happening), and there is being a Christian. Baptism relates to what happens between becoming a Christian and being a Christian. It's about the beginning of your life as a follower of Jesus. Many people say that when they were baptised something spiritual happened. That's not surprising. The Bible talks about the way in which we are spiritually linked to Jesus when we are baptised. Have a look at these two passages taken from a version of the Bible that uses up-to-date language:

'Didn't you realise we packed up and left there for good? That is what happened in baptism. *When we went under the water, we left the old country of sin behind; when we came up out of the water, we entered into the new country of grace – a new life in a new land.'* That's what baptism into the life of Jesus means. When we are lowered into the water, it is like the burial of Jesus; when we are raised up out of the water, it is like the resurrection of Jesus.' (Romans 6:2–4, *The Message* (italics added))

'If it's an initiation ritual you're after, you've already been through it by submitting to baptism. Going under the water was a burial of your old life; coming up out of it was a resurrection, God raising you from the dead as he did Christ. (Colossians 2:12, *The Message*)'

Reason 4: It pleases God

God wants people to be baptised. He spoke out loud when Jesus was baptised, confirming that Jesus was his Son, and that he was very pleased with him. If he was pleased that Jesus was baptised, he'll be equally pleased with you.

Reason 5:   We are linked with Jesus

Jesus was baptised by his cousin, John (the Baptist). John was baptising people so that they could show that they were sorry for what they had done to offend God and that they wanted to start again. Jesus (who never did anything to offend God) is the only person who never needed to be baptised for that reason, but in being baptised he identified himself with everyone else who needs to be.

When we are baptised we are doing what Jesus did (which is always a very good thing to do) and linking ourselves with him. We are saying that we are with the perfect person, even though we would never be perfect without him. It's not a bad swap is it? He shows that he wants to be with people who are imperfect and we show that we want to be with him, who is perfect.

Reason 6:   It's what Jesus wants

General John Sedgwick was an officer in the American Civil War, and on being told to keep hidden during a battle because of enemy snipers said, 'They couldn't hit an elephant at this dist...'

If you could choose them, what would you like your last words to be? Perhaps it would be something inspiring or significant. The last thing Jesus said on earth after he had been raised to life before he went back to heaven was that his followers should baptise people when they became followers. He obviously thought it was really important for it to be the last thing he said!

If we say we are followers of Jesus, and describe him as our King, our brother,

our Saviour, and our friend, we need to take it seriously when he tells us to do something. With Jesus, we always have a choice; we can say 'yes' or 'no'. But if we say 'no' then we are being disobedient.

Being baptised is a simple act of obedience to the person who has bought your life at the cost of his! Being baptised should not be a case of 'I don't feel it's right for me'. It's a command from Jesus himself, and he calls people who do what he commands 'friends':

This is my command: Love one another the way I loved you. This is the very best way to love. Put your life on the line for your friends. You are my friends when you do the things I command you. I'm no longer calling you servants because servants don't understand what their master is thinking and planning. No, I've named you friends because I've let you in on everything I've heard from the Father. (John 15:12–15, *The Message*)

So, that's six good reasons to be baptised – what reasons do you have not to?

Baptism – what happens?

'Why do we have a swimming pool in church?'

In most Baptist churches baptism is by full immersion. This basically means getting completely dunked in a big pool of water! Baptisms have taken place in rivers, the sea, swimming pools and even in an outside rubbish skip! However, most Baptist churches have a special pool for baptisms.

So why do we generally baptise people like this? Here are three good reasons why:

1 Because Jesus was baptised that way. Matthew 3:16 tells us that Jesus came up out of the river Jordan after he was baptised. If Jesus was baptised in a river then he would have got very wet! So if it is good enough for Jesus, then full immersion is good enough for anyone!

> When my Dad got baptised, all of our family came to celebrate including a load of non-Christians. My cousin was four at the time and when I was sat with him he burst out in one of the prayers, 'Claire, you should have told me there was a swimming pool in church; I haven't brought my swimming trunks!'

2 The word itself describes the action. In the original language of the New Testament, Greek, 'baptise' means dip under the water or immerse. It's a very active word, and was also used to describe a ship sinking! Get the picture?

3 It is the form of baptism that physically represents a lot of what we believe about being a Christian. It is like death and resurrection, and having a bath. Look at reason 2 in 'Why get baptised?' for more details.

The actual baptism day

'My own baptism was one of the best days of my life and one I often look back on with a huge smile! It was the best day because I was committing myself to God forever as well as having all my friends and family around me supporting me in that.'

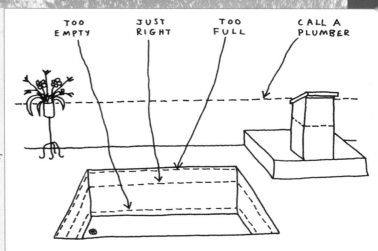

FILLING THE BAPTISTRY

Each church has different things that you need to prepare and do before and during your baptism. For example, in some churches the people being baptised have the opportunity to choose their favourite song. Here though are some common things that do happen and some words of advice!

Sharing your testimony

Many churches encourage you to prepare and share your testimony. That simply means telling people how you became a Christian and what it means to you. There is no right way to write your testimony but it may help you to answer these questions in what you say:

- How and when did you become a Christian, or realise that you are a Christian?

- What difference has being a Christian made to you (perhaps a 'before and after' summary)? (Remember this is your moment to tell all your

non-Christian friends what being a Christian really is!)

- Why are you being baptised now?
- Has God done anything special in your life?
- Which people have been significant in helping you on your journey of faith so far?

Some of you will really enjoy this moment to share your testimony; others may be scared stiff about standing up in front of so many people. The best thing is to be prepared! Have your testimony written out clearly, practise it a lot beforehand (in front of the mirror or the dog is a good idea!) and enjoy it! This is your moment to tell everyone how awesome God is and why you want to follow him. Remember, everyone is rooting for you!

Promises you will make

Before you get baptised you may be asked to declare publicly what you believe. The promises were explored in 'Exploring your faith', and will probably be something like this:

'[Your name] Do you believe in one God, Father, Son and Holy Spirit?'
(You answer) *'I do'*
'Do you confess Jesus Christ as your Lord and Saviour?'
'I do.'
'Do you turn from sin, renounce evil and intend to follow Christ?'
'I do.'
'Will you live within the fellowship of the church and will you serve Jesus Christ in the world?'
'I will'

Just before you are baptised, your minister will say something like:

'[Your name], you are called to be a disciple of Jesus Christ. I now baptise you in the name of God the Father, the Son, and the Holy Spirit. Amen'

The wet bit

Lots of people get worried about this bit. Some think they will drown, others think they will really hate being under the water. To be honest, it is over very quickly!

REMEMBER TO LET GO OF YOUR SPONSOR'S HAND BEFORE YOU ARE BAPTISED

You will probably be asked to nominate someone who will hold your towel for you (in some churches they are called your sponsor). Think carefully about who you choose, as it's a great privilege, even if it doesn't seem like a big task. This should be someone who has been a big influence in your life and in helping you to follow Jesus. As you come up out of the water your towel-holder/sponsor will pass you a towel and help you to dry your face, and perhaps they will also pray for you.

Some practical words of advice

When you get into the pool, make sure you stand so that your feet are up against the wall, or bottom of the steps. That way, you won't slip when you are leant back under the water.

Hold on tight to whoever is baptising you. If you've got them and they've got you no-one is going to leave you under the water. Agree beforehand how you will do this.

Keep your back straight and your head up. That makes it so much easier for you to be laid backwards and brought back up again. If you bend in the middle it will make it very difficult for people to lift you up.

Take a deep breath and hold it. That way

you are filled with air so actually getting you under the water is more of a problem than you drowning! Just relax, trust your minister or whoever is baptising you to look after you. Make sure you breathe in before you are tipped backwards – perhaps as you hear your minister say '...and Holy Spirit'.

Finally, the best bit of advice is to enjoy it! This is a day of celebration. You are celebrating who God is and what he has done for you. You are also telling others how much he means to you. Relax and enjoy the day!

After the wet bit

In many churches, after you have come back up you will be prayed for. This may happen while you are still standing in the water, or once you have come out. This prayer is usually a prayer that God will bless you, that he will continue to lead you, and that he will continue to make you into the person he created you to become.

Reflection activity: should I really get baptised?

Which of the following reasons are why you want get baptised? You can choose as many as you think are true, but be honest with yourself.

Because my best friend is

Because I want to follow Jesus for the rest of my life

Because I love God

Because my parents think it is a good idea

Because I have always gone to church

Because I want to obey Jesus

Because I feel it is a good idea

Because I have become a Christian

Because my youth worker asked me

Because I want to follow Jesus' example

Now tick the reasons that you believe are what God wants and cross out the wrong reasons. Is your reason still there? If it's not, perhaps you are not yet ready to be baptised – have a chat with your minister about it.

FAQs about baptism

1 Does it matter how much water is used?

Yes and no. The amount of water does not make any spiritual difference, but the physical act of immersion in water is a powerful symbol – representing death, burial and resurrection, being washed in a bath, and being immersed in the Spirit.

Not wanting to get your hair wet is not a good reason for not being baptised by immersion! However, if for medical reasons it is not possible for you to be immersed in water, water can be poured carefully over you.

2 What should I wear?

The clothes are not really important, although some churches have special baptismal robes for you to wear. If they don't then you should choose clothes that you don't mind being seen wet in. Make sure they will not go transparent, stretch embarrassingly or get really heavy and fall down when they get wet! You may want to wear a swimming costume underneath. Avoid jeans as it becomes difficult to walk in them when they get wet! Try to make sure that the colour won't run out of them too! It is a good idea to have a test run in your bath or shower a couple of days beforehand.

If you wear glasses it would be wise to keep them on as you go into the pool so that you can see where you are going, and then hand them to someone to keep safe until after you have been baptised.

WHAT NOT TO WEAR FOR YOUR BAPTISM

ARMOUR (TOO HEAVY)

THIN T-SHIRT (TOO SEE-THROUGH)

RUBBER RING (TOO BUOYANT)

RABBIT COSTUME (TOO FLUFFY)

3   Do I have to give my testimony?

It would be a real shame if you don't. Giving a testimony is a significant part of what you do because it's your chance to tell everyone in your own words why you're being baptised. It is also helpful for people who are there who are either not yet Christians or not yet baptised, so they can hear why you are now a believer and being baptised.

It would be worth writing out your testimony in full, even if you don't intend to read it out. That way you can always remember what you wanted to say if you forget what you were saying. If you're feeling nervous about giving your testimony in front of everyone, remember that they are all there to support you, they are rooting for you!

In some churches, instead of standing up on your own someone might interview you. A last resort may be to ask someone else to read your testimony.

4 What should I say in my testimony?

You don't have to tell your whole life history in detail. It may help you to answer these questions in what you say:

- How and when did you become a Christian, or realise that you are a Christian?
- What difference has being a Christian made to you (perhaps a 'before and after' summary)?
- Why are you being baptised now?
- Has God done anything special in your life?
- Which people have been significant in helping you on your journey of faith so far?

5 Who can baptise me?

It doesn't have to be a minister (if your church has one) although it is often helpful if a minister is involved as they will have experience and training in what to do. In some churches there may be two people in the pool with you to make the physics of the event easier. They may both be church leaders, however some churches may allow you to invite someone you choose to be in the pool.

You will usually be advised to choose someone to sit with you during the service and to hold your towel during the baptism. This can be anyone you choose, but think carefully: it may seem like an insignificant task but many people consider it an honour – who would you like to thank or bless by asking them to be a part of your baptism?

6 How old do I have to be?

Baptist churches do not usually have a strict age limit on when you can be baptised. However, most churches will want to make sure that you have a

mature faith and understanding of what you are doing, which is why you may have been told to wait if you have asked to be baptised when you were younger. Generally it is considered to be better to wait than be baptised without understanding fully what you are doing.

7   What if my parents don't want me to be baptised?

This is a tough decision. The Bible tells us that we have to honour and obey our parents, but it also says that following Jesus and doing what he wants should be the most important thing in our lives. You will have to make the final decision, but it may help you to think a bit more about these issues:

- When the Bible says that children should obey their parents in everything because it pleases God (look at Colossians 3:20) it is possible that Paul was writing about a situation where they were Christian parents. However, the fifth commandment speaks of honouring your parents and there is no comment about whether or not they worship God.

- Jesus said that we can't be his disciple if we love our parents more than him (read Luke 14:26), but he also stressed that obeying the fifth commandment was important too (have a look at Luke 18:20). Balancing the two principles in this case is difficult, but remember that Jesus was not saying we should not love our parents, just that he should be first.

- Is this a battle worth fighting? Will your parents be more impressed by your strength of faith if you go ahead against their wishes because you want to obey God, or by you saying that you will respect their wishes until you are older?

- Why don't your parents want you to be baptised? Is it because they oppose your faith, or is it because they don't think you are 'ready'? Are they saying, 'No!' or are they saying, 'Not yet'?

8   What if I have been christened/baptised as a baby?

You're not the first person to ask this – baptism was one of the issues that led the earliest Baptists to leave the established church. While these Baptists were accused of 'rebaptising' those who had been baptised as infants, they did not see themselves as doing this at all. In their view infant baptism was not valid because it was not the result of a freely chosen decision to believe.

You will need to think through very carefully with the help of others what to do if you were baptised as a baby. Talk with your parents if appropriate and your minister. There is no rule stopping you from being baptised as a believer if you have been christened, but it is not a decision to be taken lightly. Some discover that they can value what happened to them as a child and the promises made by parents on their behalf, and perhaps decide to have a service where they can reaffirm those promises for themselves. Others will sense that to be baptised as a believer is the right step to take for them.

9   What if I have been confirmed?

Confirmation is when you affirm publicly for yourself the vows that were made on your behalf when you were christened. For some Christians this is a significant spiritual moment in their life and they do not feel the need to be baptised as a believer. For others, their confirmation was something they did because it was expected of them or because others were being confirmed and the event did not mean anything special to them. Still others would say that even though they were confirmed they were not actually believers at the time.

If you are in either of the second or third groups you may well want to be baptised as a believer now. If you are in the first group you might not want to be baptised as a believer now because you say that you have had a baptism and a public declaration of your faith in Jesus, although they were separated by a few years. Again, a special service where you affirm the promises you made at your confirmation is possible. In either case you'll need to talk this through very carefully with your parents and minister, recognising that while there's no rule saying that you can't be baptised as a believer if you have been confirmed, the promises you made at your confirmation are a very special commitment to have made.

Joining the church

Baptism and church membership

'Your body has many parts – limbs, organs, cells – but no matter how many parts you can name, you're still one body. It's exactly the same with Christ. By means of his one Spirit, we all said goodbye to our partial and piecemeal lives. We each used to independently call our own shots, but then we entered into a large and integrated life in which he has the final say in everything. (This is what we proclaimed in word and action when we were baptised).'
(1 Corinthians 12:12–13 *The Message*)

Introduction

There is a close link between baptism and church membership and in most cases those being baptised will be received into membership shortly afterwards. This may be either immediately after the baptism as part of the same service or at a separate 'welcome service' on another occasion. Whichever is the case membership follows baptism and something which we see happening in the early church. Check out Acts 2:41–47 where the believers who were being baptised joined with the other believers as church.

In many ways being baptised is our entry into the church. When someone becomes a Christian and is then baptised as a believer they became part of the church of Jesus Christ – along with all the other Christians on the planet! Being part of the church worldwide is great. If you hadn't realised, it's not just you and

few others who believe this stuff but around two billion others do too (that's about one third of the world's population!). It means that almost anywhere you go on your travels you could find a group of believers meeting together as church, and could join them for worship (even if you don't speak their language!).

However, being committed to the church worldwide isn't easy, if at all possible, and in practice belonging a 'local church' means that we can much more easily be part of things – to get the support of other Christians, be involved in the life and work the church, and demonstrate commitment to one another. That is why membership of a local church goes hand in hand with baptism. In this section we'll explore why church is important to us as Christians and in particular what it means to be a member of a Baptist church.

What is church?

It all started in a very small way, with a small group of confused believers but with a BIG God – Father, Son and Holy Spirit – the church has spread right around the world, and is still doing so today.

Being a Christian is not only about your personal faith and acceptance of Jesus Christ as Lord and Saviour but also involves us becoming part of his church. In the Bible, church is described in a number of different ways – here are three aspects of church that we see there...

'A gathering of worshippers'

It is possible to worship and pray to God on our own and this is an important part of life as a follower of Jesus, but there is something special that takes place when we gather together in Jesus' name to worship him. (Read Psalm 92:1–3; Psalm 96:1–6 and Matthew 18:20)

Family of God

As followers of Jesus we are all brothers and sisters in Christ, making us one BIG family. Family is a good thing to be part of (part of God's design for life!) but just like we can't choose our natural family members it does also mean that we can't choose who we want to be in our church. Instead we must love all of our Christian brothers and sisters. (Read 1 John 4:19–5:1)

Body of Christ

In his letters to the early believers the Apostle Paul describes the church as being a bit like a person's body. (Look at 1 Corinthians 12:12–27)

The human body is made up of many different parts that all fit together to make it complete and in the same way the church is made up of different people who all fit together. Jesus is 'the head of his body, the church' and 'under his direction the whole body is healthy and growing and full of love' (see Ephesians 4:15–16). In other words we're not all the same – but bring different gifts to make up the church as we seek to follow Jesus together.

In summing up, church is the people of God (not the building we meet in) and as Christians we need the church and the church needs us. What's more, Jesus loves the church and his prayer is that it works together to glorify God and to show his love to the world. (Check out John 17 for Jesus' prayer, remembering that he prayed this just before he was arrested!)

What gifts do you think God has given you to use as part of the church? The answer can't be none – God has given us all different gifts to use (look at Romans 12:6). Take time in the lead up to your baptism to think about this and ask God to start to show you what these gifts might be – don't just think of jobs that need doing on a Sunday morning!

But why are there so many different churches?

Denomination is the name for a particular type of church or group of churches – and there are certainly lots of different ones. In most towns (or even villages) there is probably a good selection of different churches, represented by different church buildings – and there may be others that can't be spotted in the High Street as they meet in a school or village hall or even in someone's home.

If you enjoy anagrams see if you can work out some of these – they're all fairly well known Christian denominations...
Answers are below

Canal gin

Anatomy rivals

Cleanest pot

A chic lot

Modest hit

Past bit

Ox Hotrod

Refund More Diet

Rent herb

Anglican, Salvation Army, Pentecostal, Catholic, Methodist, Baptist, Orthodox, United Reformed, Brethren

As with the anagrams it can all get a bit confusing as to what different denominations believe or how they 'do church', but the main thing to remember is that all Christian denominations, whether traditional ones or 'new churches', believe the same main things about God, Jesus and the Holy Spirit found in the Bible and in many different ways there is a lot of working together between the different denominations locally, nationally and internationally. After all we are all one church! It's a little bit like the British Army. There are different regiments with different traditions, and some have expertise in different areas of 'armying'. But they all fight on the same side.

Look back to the 'Exploring Your Faith' section if you need a re-cap on key beliefs of Christians.

So what is distinctive about Baptist churches?

The answer to this might appear to be a fairly simple one – believers' baptism. Baptist Christians believe that baptism should be for those who have made a decision for themselves to follow Jesus and be baptised. We speak of 'believers' baptism' to show this, rather than 'adult baptism'. Baptist believers are usually baptised by full immersion (ie being completely dunked in a big pool of water!).

As with a number of other denominations down through the history of the church, Baptist churches began with a 'breakaway group' of Christians that disagreed with aspects of the traditional church. They believed the church should be made up of believers, and

What do you think is different about Baptist churches?

so committed to baptise only those who could make a confession of faith in Jesus as Lord for themselves. This was very different from the normal practice of baptising infants. It was saying that baptism was an important step of repentance, faith and obedience for the believer to take. From this radical beginning arose the Baptist denomination we have today.

Other distinctives of Baptist churches are:

We believe the Bible is 'the Word of God', so there is a strong emphasis placed on teaching from the Bible.

We believe that God speaks to and through everyone (not just ministers, priests or vicars) – and so we make decisions together as the gathered church; this gathering is usually called the 'church meeting'. Church meetings are sometimes thought of as being like business meetings, but they should be far more than that: they are places where God's people try to work out what he wants them to be doing.

Each local Baptist church appoints its own leaders. Some have ministers to serve the church and take responsibility for things like preaching, teaching and looking after people in the church. Baptist churches also usually have teams of leaders – sometimes called deacons (and sometimes elders) who are there to help the church function, and they are appointed by the church meeting. There

is no hierarchy of bishops or priests, but many Baptist churches in this country are linked together through the Baptist Union of Great Britain.

We believe that everyone in the church has an equal and necessary role to play (it's not just down to the leaders) – and so all are encouraged to find and take up that role serving God in the life and mission of the local church.

We believe that every believer should share their faith with others.

Other denominations and churches may share some or all of these principles and practices, but not in quite the same way. Baptist churches also talk of having Five Core Values: they are worshipping communities, inclusive communities, missionary communities, prophetic communities and sacrificial communities.

What do you think the Five Core Values mean? You can find out more at www.baptist.org.uk

Why do we have church members?

As mentioned earlier, knowing that we belong to the worldwide family of God's people is great but in practice this is hard to relate to. Becoming a member of a local church is about formalising the fact that we've become a 'member' of the body of Christ when we became a Christian (remember 1 Corinthians 12?) and making a commitment to a group of believers in a particular place (remember Acts 2:41–42?).

If everyone is welcome in a church, why are some people church members and not others?

For the local church, having a committed membership means that:

We have a clear idea of those who are believers and seeking to serve him with us.

We can better support, care and look out for one another.

We are committed to supporting the work of the church through giving time, gifts, prayers and money.

We can gather together before God to make decisions about the running of the church.

Ultimately it means that we can work together more easily to fulfil the mission of God in our locality.

What does being a church member mean in practice?

Being a church member should certainly mean more than just 'turning up' on a Sunday (or whatever day of the week there's a meeting!). As a church member participation in the life and direction of the church is vital. As we said earlier, a distinctive of Baptist churches is that all members have an equal and necessary part to play in the life and mission of the local church and in that sense everyone is needed to make the church effective (remember Paul's 'body parts'?). If we look again at Acts chapter 2 we can see a number of things that were important to the early believers – and these continue to be important to us as we join together as believers today.

Worship

Have another look at Acts 2:41–47; what significant things did the believers do together?

Meeting together to worship God is important for all of us, as well as honouring to God. Whether we feel like it or not God is always worthy of our worship and when we gather together in Jesus' name we gain a greater sense of the presence of God among us. Meeting together for times of worship, teaching, breaking bread (communion) and prayer should also be times to encourage and build one another up in Christ.

What is important about meeting together with other Christians? Check out Hebrews 10:23–26; the writer of Hebrews had a lot to say about the importance of meeting together.

If we believe that God is able to speak to and through all those who are part of the church, it is important that all are involved, before God, in making decisions about the direction and running of the church: seeking and understanding God's will for the church as well as practical matters.

THERE ARE OCCASIONS WHEN EVERYONE AGREES IN CHURCH MEETINGS

One function of the church meeting is to appoint those who serve in the church as ministers, deacons and other leaders. It would also be the place where it is agreed to welcome new members into the church. Part of the church meeting should be given over to praying together for the church, its membership, life and mission in the locality.

Note: In some Baptist churches young people may have to be of a certain age before being received into church membership or allowed to attend church meetings (16 or 18 years old). Other churches welcome young people into membership after baptism without age limit but until they are 18 years old would not expect them to take on the full responsibilities of church membership (ie attending church meetings) as this may only add to the pressure faced by many teens. Instead they are encouraged to take a full part in the youth programme as well as beginning to serve the church in other ways. Young members may also be encouraged to attend church meetings which have particular relevance to them (such as the appointment of a youth worker).

Do you have any questions about how your church is run? Is this all a bit confusing? Jot down any questions you have and ask your youth leader/minister next time you meet.

Mission

Mission describes activities that we engage in that look out beyond the walls of the church. Both telling people about Jesus and meeting people's needs are aspects of mission. This may be through organised events or activities (anything from preaching on

Are you currently involved in the mission of your church? In what ways? If the answer's no – ask God to show you how you can be effective in sharing your faith.

the street to washing people's cars!) or more simply through our relationships with non-Christians around us. It may also involve the supporting of those working as missionaries in other places.

Finances

Local Baptist churches are responsible for their own finances and rely on the regular giving of those in membership for the activities and expenses of the church. Aside from the need for finance to run the church, it is also considered part of our worship that we give back to God some of what he has given to us.

How do you use the money you have (assuming you have at least some!)? How could you make this an act of worship to God? What about the things you own – how can you make using them an act of worship too?

Some Baptist churches encourage members to *tithe* their income – a Biblical principle where God's people gave back to God the best 10% of all they produced. When giving your tithe or any offering, you are not giving it to the church or to support a particular person but giving to God.

How am I welcomed into church membership?

Ahead of your baptismal/welcome service your name will be brought to the church meeting and the person(s) preparing you for baptism will usually give a short report and recommendation that you are received into membership following your baptism. No need to worry too much – it's unlikely they'll turn you down!!

As mentioned earlier you may then be received into membership as part of your baptismal service or alternatively at a separate 'welcome service' – it depends on the usual practice of your church, but will usually be followed by the breaking of bread (or communion).

The order of service and the words used (as with your baptism) will vary from church to church but the general format will include:

- You will be asked questions, where you make a commitment to serving God in your local church.
- The church congregation will then be invited to stand and will make a similar promise to you.
- You will then be welcomed by those at the front with a handshake or a hug!
- Prayers will be said for you as you take up your place as a member of the church.
- The breaking of bread (or communion) part of the service often follows, where you will share in the bread and the wine for the first time as a church member!